First published in Great Britain 2021 by Farshore

An imprint of HarperCollins*Publishers*
1 London Bridge Street, London SE1 9GF
www.farshore.co.uk

HarperCollins*Publishers*
1st Floor, Watermarque Building, Ringsend Road
Dublin 4, Ireland

Written by Emily Stead.
Designed by Grant Kempster.
Cover designed by Jessica Coomber.

ISBN 978 0 7555 0185 4
Printed in UK
5

BRAIN TEASERS

Welcome to Galar ...
the latest known region in the
world of Pokémon!

On an island that's bursting with lore
and legend, you'll meet a host of newly
discovered Pokémon – from the mischievous
to the mysterious!

Challenge yourself to become the best Trainer
you can be by tackling the tough brain teasers,
testing riddles and tricky number challenges
on the pages that follow.

Try your best, Trainer!

Sparks fly when this fierce fire-breather soars into town!
Rearrange the letters below, using each letter only once,
to reveal the Pokémon's name.

D R C
A Z H R
I
A

- - - - - - - - - - - -

Now make ten more words of three letters or more using
any of the letters above only once.

•   •

•   •

•   •

•   •

•   •

THAT'S THE SPIRIT!

DIFFICULTY:

If you see this terrifying trio of Ghost-type Pokémon – run fast! Circle the correct shadow for each critter before they spirit you away!

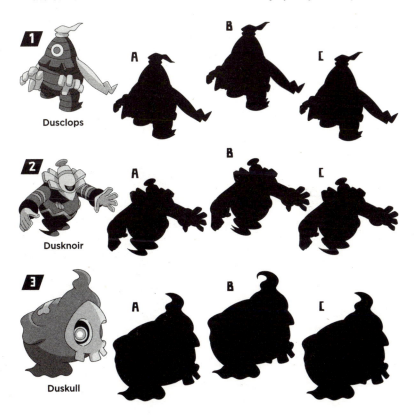

1 Dusclops — A, B, C

2 Dusknoir — A, B, C

3 Duskull — A, B, C

Now sort the Pokémon into the order of their Evolution.

1 . . . .

2 . . . .

3 . . . .

PIKACHU'S PUZZLE

Which three electrifying moves should Pikachu use in its next battle? Fill in the missing letters to crack the code, then work out the secret message below. Three letters have been filled in for you.

A	B	C	D	E	F	G	H	I
	25							

J	K	L	M	N	O	P	Q	R
	8					13		

S	T	U	V	W	X	Y	Z

__ __ __ __ __ __ __
13 6 8 24 26 5 18

__ __ __ __ __ __
16 5 12 18 9 1

__ __ __　__ __ __ __ __　__ __ __ __ __ __
18 16 2　14 18 6 26 8　24 17 17 24 26 8

__ __ __ __　__ __ __ __　__ __ __
6 13 12 11　17 24 6 9　24 11 1

__ __ __ __ __ __ __ __ __ __ __.
17 5 18 11 1 2 15 25 12 9 17

FEELING SQUARE

This Galarian gaggle adds up to a whole heap of trouble!
Work out the totals for the three Pokémon in each column
and row using the key to help you.

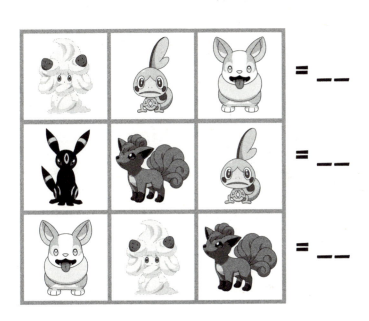

CRITTER COMBAT

When these two Pokémon go head-to-head, you had better stand back! Read the riddle clues to unravel a secret word.

My first is in BUG
and also in BERRY.

My second is in ULTRA
and also in ASH.

My third begins TOGEPI,
TYRANITAR too.

My fourth ends both
RUFFLET and SWOOBAT.

My fifth is in GALAR
and twice in GALLADE.

My sixth is in FEEBAS
and also in EEVEE.

Think you've solved the riddle?
Write your answer, then see:

— — — — — —

GOLDEN SLUMBERS

Sleepy Snorlax can snooze anywhere! Unscramble the names of five places where he likes to nap.

1. E N D _ _ _

2. V A E C _ _ _ _ _

3. E E R T _ _ _ _ _

4. W U B R O R _ _ _ _ _ _ _

5. S T E N _ _ _ _

QUICK QUIZ

Circle the Pokémon from which Snorlax evolves.

CRATES COUNT

DIFFICULTY:

The villainous Team Rocket are storing crates to transport stolen Pokémon. How many crates has Meowth collected so far?

= • • • • • • •

James delivers more crates – how many do Team Rocket have now?

= • • • • • • •

12

NINETALES' NUMBERS

Fill each shaded square with the numbers 1 to 9 – the same number of tails belonging to the famous Fire-type Pokémon, Ninetales! Make sure that each row and column contain the numbers 1-9 only once.

PUZZLE 1

DIFFICULTY: EASY

	8	4	6		5		2	9
9		5			4	3		6
2	6		9	3		8	4	
		6		2			8	4
8	9		4	6	1		3	7
	4	3	8	5			6	
5	1	8	3		6		7	
6	3	7		4	2		9	8
4		9		7			5	

PUZZLE 2

DIFFICULTY: TOUGH

	8	4	6		5		2	9
9		5			4	3		6
2	6		9	3		8	4	
		6		2			8	
8	9		4	6	1		3	7
	4	3	8	5			6	
5	1	8	3		6		7	
6	3	7		4	2		9	8
4		9		7			5	

TREE CLIMB

Here's a tough challenge that may stump you! Start at the bottom of each tree, then work out the calculations as you climb up. Write the final answer at the top of each tree.

Tree 1:
+27
−4
×3
÷2
18

Tree 2:
−4
×8
÷6
+16
50

Tree 3:
+9
−46
÷2
×100
8

WHO'S THAT POKÉMON?

Which speedy climber is pictured above? Write its name below, then tick which type it belongs to.

A. Ground ☐   B. Bug ☐   C. Grass ☐

MIRRORED MESSAGE

Uh-oh, it looks like Rotom needs a reboot! Use a mirror to work out Rotom's flipped-out message, then write out the words below.

ON THE DOUBLE

There are eight differences between the pictures of this Galarian group. How many can you spy? Circle the changes as you find them.

MEGA MORPH

Time for your next brainpower boost, Trainer! Change the word 'JOLT' into 'FAST' in five quick steps, using the clues to help you. You must change only one letter to make a new word at each step without rearranging the other letters – for example, BALL could become BAIL.

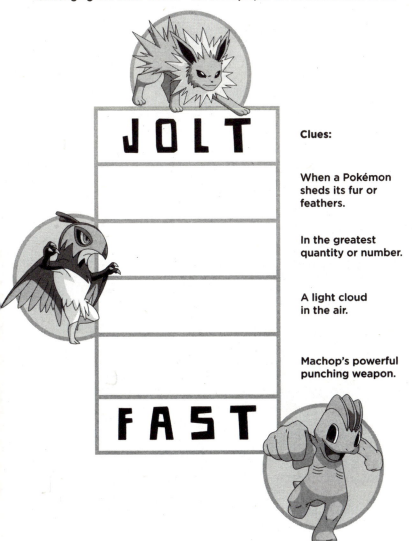

JOLT

FAST

Clues:

When a Pokémon sheds its fur or feathers.

In the greatest quantity or number.

A light cloud in the air.

Machop's powerful punching weapon.

GROWING UP

Pokémon are such fascinating creatures! They are growing and
changing all the time! Write the letters in the boxes to show
the correct order of the Evolution chains.

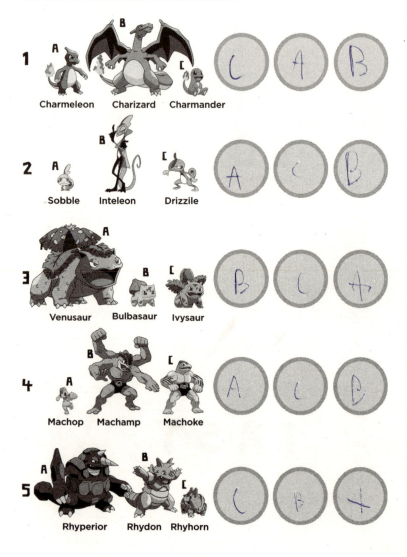

1
Charmeleon   Charizard   Charmander

C   A   B

2
Sobble   Inteleon   Drizzile

A   C   B

3
Venusaur   Bulbasaur   Ivysaur

B   C   A

4
Machop   Machamp   Machoke

A   C   B

5
Rhyperior   Rhydon   Rhyhorn

C   B   A

PSYCHIC POWERS

Read the clues and study the pictures to help you place all the names of the powerful Psychic-type Pokémon into the grid below.

Meowstic
Espurr
Espeon
Swoobat
Gardevoir
Gallade
Woobat
Mewtwo

ACROSS

2. A creature that shares its DNA with the mighty Mew.
5. Conceals its psychic powers on the insides of its ears.
6. Has a special orb on its head and evolves from Eevee.
7. A graceful Pokémon that has the power to read the future.

DOWN

1. A Psychic- and Fighting-type, one of Ralts' final forms.
3. The fluttering Bat Pokémon with a heart-shaped nose.
4. Emitting powerful sound waves tires out this Pokémon.
6. This Psychic-type has a blank expression that never changes.

19

Start at the letter A, then guide this hungry Bulbasaur through the grid in alphabetical order to find a tasty Berry.

WHO'S THAT POKÉMON?

As Bulbasaur soaks up the sun's rays, the seed on its back grows and grows until it's time to evolve! Fill in the missing letters to reveal the names of both Evolutions.

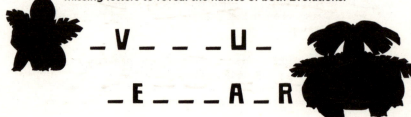

_ V _ _ _ U _

_ E _ _ _ A _ R

DIFFICULTY:

As day turns to dusk, a host of Pokémon are hiding in plain sight.
Write down the coordinates when you spot each concealed creature.
To get you started, Woobat is in square B7.

Woobat B 7

Larvitar B 3

Braviary D G

Dusclops G 1

Mimikyu E 2

Onix F 5

TRUE PATH

Begin at the START, then hop across the Poké Balls landing only on the genuine ones. Leap wisely, Trainer, there's only one correct route to the FINISH.

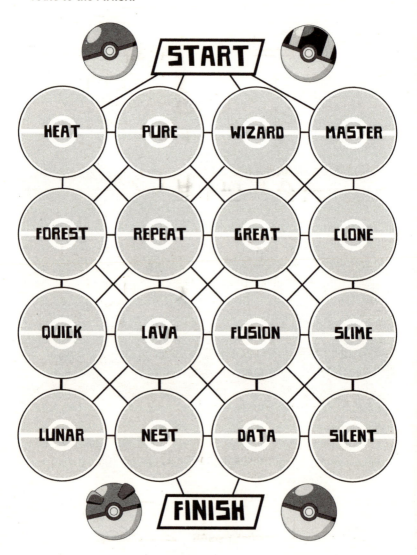

22

WEIGHT WORK OUT

It's time for the grand Pokémon weigh in! Read the weight on each scale, then work out how much Snorlax, Munchlax and Pikachu weigh separately.

Pikachu weighs:	_____ kg
Munchlax weighs:	_____ kg
Snorlax weighs:	_____ kg

23

TALKING IN RIDDLES

DIFFICULTY:

Will this Poké Ball riddle leave you feeling puffed up with pride or pretty perplexed? Write the letters from each clue below to reveal Ash's chosen Poké Ball.

My first begins MEW
and MEWTWO, too.

My second is in GRASS
and also in WATER.

My third is in NEST BALL
but never in NET BALL.

My fourth is in STEEL
and also in ULTRA.

My fifth begins EGG
and EVOLUTION.

My sixth is in DARK
but never in OAK.

Write your answer below – it's no time to joke!

— — — — — —

DIFFICULTY:

Find the names of a dozen Pokémon that hail from the Galar region in the Poké Ball below. The names read forwards, backwards, up, down and diagonally.

```
              R I D J Y U P G Q S P
            P T Z K W O Q R E Y T I G
          S H N D V T M O L L H J D X E B W
          B G U C U R B N D T G M C A V L Y
        A Y V U L P I X E V J E Z W P X D O J
        O R T Q S B A J H G B I L O X V T Q N G R
        Z C N I E G H P W M C H P H N S B U X U Z
      L E A F E O N Q R B H M E L I C D R D G K D B
      Q C N B J D Y L O Q B G U E O S H J P E S J V
      G Z I U T P N U C E      B V I Y F O Q W O O
      Y H N Q E B N Q Z R      H R E A R G Y O N I
      D O E S R A U N K V      C S G E W X S O G R
      V T B W C H B L S N U P M U Y I O Q N H B S T
      P Z H V P G R J I R T L O X B K P M J Z A T H
      M E W T W O N E U W H G H I S E C N Y T D
      I D H S U C G V F Y O T C G N S R L O U Q
        N T Q P S X Q F U G P V B W O P B W C
          Z U N W B J L H Z D I O H S A Y Q
          Y E D L A V E O N U Q Y T O V U D
            O B H Y M T P H B H L D J E H
              M Y L T S A G R X N C Y R
```

ARCANINE	LEAFEON	RUFFLET
EEVEE	MEWTWO	SCORBUNNY
GASTLY	ONIX	SWOOBAT
JOLTEON	RHYHORN	VULPIX

WHO'S THAT POKÉMON?

Which little Pokémon is hiding at the centre of the grid? Write its name below, then tick which type it belongs to.

- - - - - - - - -

A. Fire ☐   **B.** Dragon ☐   **C.** Dark ☐

A FAIR FIGHT

Fill in the missing letters of these fierce Fighting-type Pokémon. Check out the close-up clues if you get stuck.

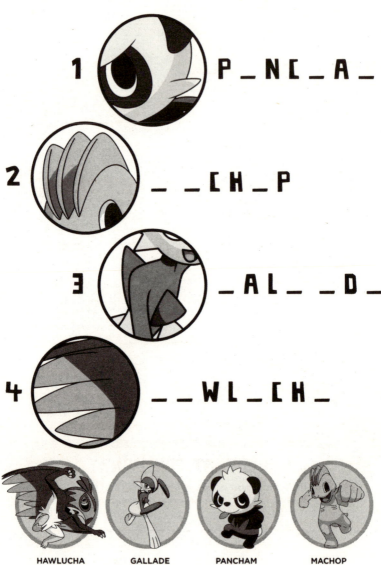

1 P _ N C _ A _

2 _ _ C H _ P

3 _ A L _ _ D _

4 _ _ W L _ C H _

HAWLUCHA   GALLADE   PANCHAM   MACHOP

ON THE ATTACK

Only top Trainers can defeat Onix, the Rock Snake Pokémon.
Escape Onix's awesome attack by placing the letters O, N, I
and X once in every row, column and 2x2 box.

PUZZLE 1

DIFFICULTY: EASY

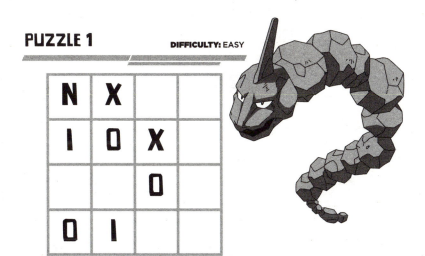

N	X		
I	O	X	
		O	
O	I		

PUZZLE 2

DIFFICULTY: TOUGH

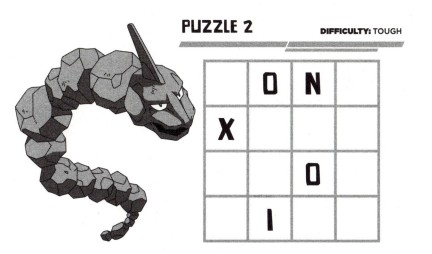

	O	N	
X			
		O	
	I		

A GASTLY PUZZLE

Gastly has a gaseous body, like the gas molecules in the picture below. Arrange the numbers 1, 2, 3, 4, 5, 6 and 7 in the circles so that each straight line of three numbers adds up to the same total. You can use each number only once.

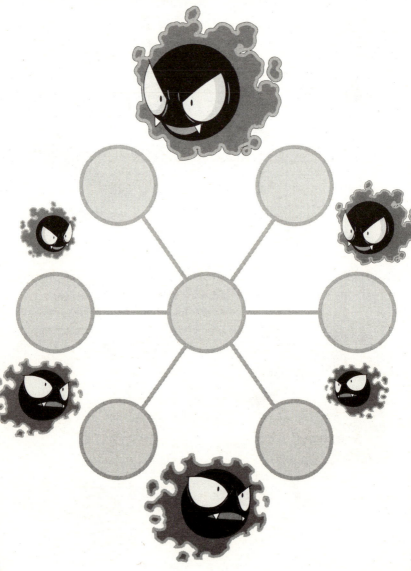

GRIDLOCKED

How well do you know your Water-type Pokémon? Fit the names of the ten super splashers below into the grid. Tip: try starting with the Pokémon with the longest names first.

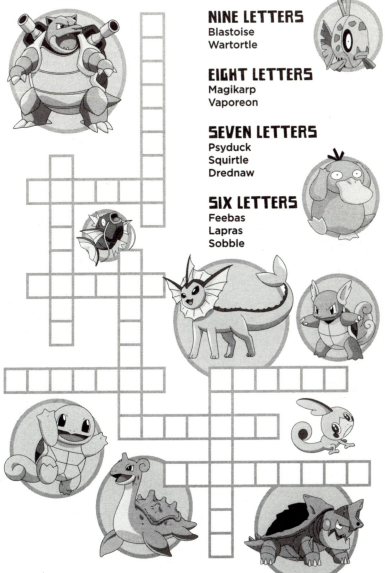

NINE LETTERS
Blastoise
Wartortle

EIGHT LETTERS
Magikarp
Vaporeon

SEVEN LETTERS
Psyduck
Squirtle
Drednaw

SIX LETTERS
Feebas
Lapras
Sobble

Jessie has challenged you to a battle! She opens with her meddlesome Meowth. Crack the coded message to reveal the brave battler that will help you overcome the Scratch Cat Pokémon.

A	B	C	D	E	F	G	H	I
						T		

J	K	L	M	N	O	P	Q	R
			N					

S	T	U	V	W	X	Y	Z
				D		B	

N V L D G S   X Z M   Y V

W V U V Z G V W   Y B

X S V V H R M T   Z

U R T S G R N T   G B K V

K L P V N L M.

TRIPLE TEST

DIFFICULTY: ⊙⊙

Here's a trio of trials for you, Trainer! Test how sharp your sudoku skills are with these type element puzzles. Draw the elements in the grids so that each column and row contains only one of each type.

PUZZLE 1
DIFFICULTY: EASY

PUZZLE 2
DIFFICULTY: TOUGH

PUZZLE 3
DIFFICULTY: SUPER TOUGH

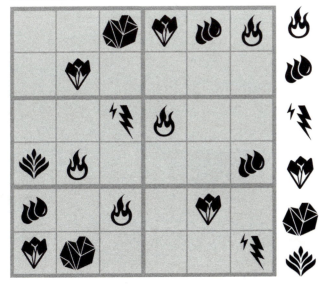

HIGH FLYER

Only eagle-eyed Trainers will be able to work out the name
of this fearsome flyer! Try to solve the anagram in your head
before tracing the paths.

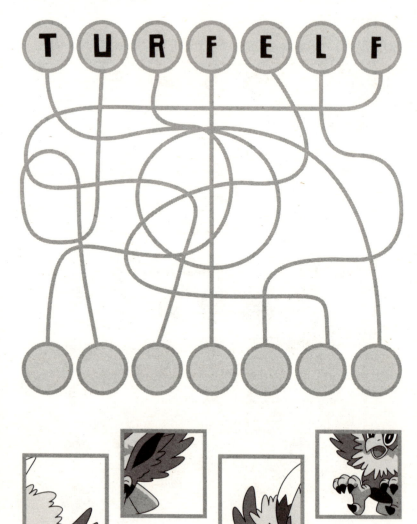

T U R F E L F

32

This cute creature would be perfectly symmetrical but for five differences. Circle five differences on the right half of the picture.

Unscramble the name of the famous Pokémon before it flutters on by.

TERBUEFTER

- - - - - - - - - -

Now tick which type it belongs to.

Bug- and Flying-type ☐   or Normal- and Flying-type ☐

ELECTRIC DREAMS

Help this sparky Joltik power up to become an electrifying Galvantula!
Fill in the missing numbers in the grid from 1 to 25 in order, then trace
a path to complete the electrical circuit. Take care, though, one wrong
move could break the circuit! Use only horizontal and vertical lines.

Example solution:

6	7	10	11
5	8	9	12
4	3	14	13
1	2	15	16

	20	21		25
		8		24
	10	7	6	
16		12	3	4
15	14	13		1

34

SWORN ENEMIES

Sly Jessie and kind Ash are opposites in every way! Change the word 'MEAN' into 'GOOD' in four steps, using the clues to help you. Change only one letter to make a new word at each step without rearranging the other letters – for example, DARK could become DART.

MEAN
GOOD

Clues:

To complain or grumble about something.

These can appear in crescent, half or full forms.

How someone is feeling or their state of mind.

35

IN THE DARK

Just one of these shadows was cast by the Dark- and Dragon-type Pokémon, but which? Choose carefully, Trainer.

Now unscramble the name of the short-sighted creature.

I O D N E D E

_ _ _ _ _ _

WHO'S WHO?

Six fine Flying-type Pokémon soar on Galar's skyline. But can you tell these formidable flyers apart? Work out who's who from the clues and pictures.

1 As the name suggests, it's a proud and heroic flyer.

2 This Pokémon reigns supreme in the region's skies.

3 A powerful young Pokémon that likes to ruffle feathers!

4 This wingless wonder can surprisingly be seen in the skies.

5 Known as the Wrestling Pokémon, it's a bit of a showboater.

6 This critter hangs out in dark forests and caves.

ODD TYPE OUT

Could your Pokémon knowledge rival the Rotom Dex's?
Find out by completing this next puzzle. Circle the creature
that's a different type from the others in each row.

1   Ninetales   Dusknoir   Arcanine   Charmeleon   Flareon

2   Riolu   Pancham   Machoke   Alcremie   Machop

3   Sobble   Grookey   Wartortle   Vaporeon   Squirtle

4   Espeon   Wooloo   Snorlax   Eevee   Munchlax

5   Yamper   Raichu   Jolteon   Jigglypuff   Meowth

TRIANGLE TEST

Happy little Togepi thinks triangles are the best shapes ever!
How many triangles can you spot in each puzzle below?
Count them up, then write down the triangle totals.

PUZZLE 1

PUZZLE 2

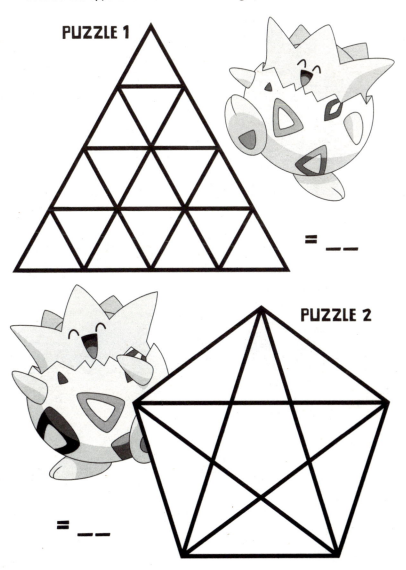

= __

= __

CHAIN REACTION

More changing creatures, but just how do they evolve?
Write the letters in the boxes to show the Evolution chains.

1
B
C
A
Squirtle   Blastoise   Wartortle

2
A
B
C
Butterfree   Metapod   Caterpie

3
A
B
C
Pikachu   Pichu   Riachu

4
A
B
C
Haunter   Gengar   Gastly

5
A
B
C
Hydreigon   Deino   Zweilous

WINGED WONDER

Certain types of Pokémon in the Galar region should be approached with caution. Unravel the riddle to reveal the type of these dangerous Pokémon.

My first is in PSYDUCK and also in DEINO.

My second begins RALTS and RIOLU, too.

My third is in JAMES but never in JESSIE.

My fourth is in GHOST and also in GRASS.

My fifth is in ONIX and also in DUSCLOPS.

My sixth ends UMBREON and VAPOREON too.

Write down the answer, when you've solved each clue:

_ _ _ _ _ _

41

LEGEND HAS IT

If you come across this Legendary Pokémon, you can count yourself super lucky, Trainer! Rejig the letters below, using each letter just once, to reveal the Pokémon's name.

- - - - - - - - - -

Now make ten more words of three letters or more using any of the letters above only once.

· ·

· ·

· ·

· ·

· ·

IN A TANGLE

Follow the paths to reveal the name of a frosty Ice-type Pokémon.
Try to solve the anagram in your head before tracing the paths!

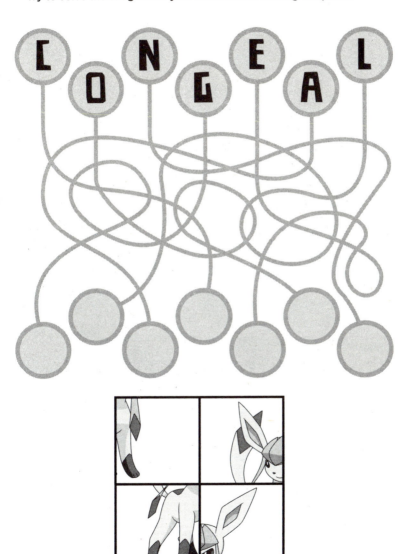

FIRST CATCH

Ash is aiming to make a special catch! Guide him through the maze in alphabetical order, then fill in the missing letters below to reveal which Pokémon is the catch of the day!

M _ _ H O _

To make his next catch, Ash needs to go backwards! Start at the letter Z and find a path to the Pokémon in reverse alphabetical order.

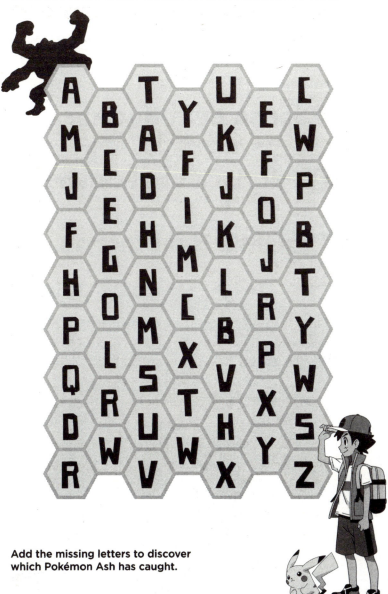

Add the missing letters to discover which Pokémon Ash has caught.

_ _ C _ A _ _

RACE DAY

Super swimmers Lapras, Magikarp, Psyduck and Squirtle have raced through the waves to shore. The watery Pokémon finished as follows:

1 Lapras beat Magikarp.

2 Psyduck beat Squirtle.

3 Squirtle beat Lapras.

Who came first in the race?

. . . .

LEAFEON'S TEST

Fail Leafeon's test and you must take your leave from Galar!
Using the numbers at the bottom of the page once only, make
the three numbers in every leaf above add up to 21.

11

10

6

5

4

3

1

2

12

9

14

8

13

7

RAVEN RIDE

This red-eyed Raven Pokémon is the best airborne taxi service in Galar! Unscramble the Pokémon's name and write it below.

K I T V I R G N O H C

– – – – – – – – – – –

All of the noble words below contain the word KNIGHT, but one is an imposter! Cross out the one that isn't a true and worthy word.

KNIGHTHOOD

KNIGHTLY

UNKNIGHT

KNIGHTLINESS

UKNIGHTED

WEEKNIGHT

BEKNIGHT

On his journey to become a Pokémon Master, Ash has faced many extraordinary challenges. Can you change 'HERO' to 'FEAT' in just five steps? Remember to change only one letter to make a new word at each step. Use the clues to help you.

H E R O

Clues:

A group of farmed Pokémon.

Where you place a hat.

To receive sound through your ears.

A feeling of worry or terror.

F E A T

CRITTER CHALLENGE

The view through Ash's telescope reveals some rare Pokémon!
Draw TWO straight lines to divide the circle into four sections –
each section should contain:

- One Grookey
- One Scorbunny
- One Sobble

Rules:
1. The lines may cross each other.
2. The lines must touch the circle edges.

FULL CIRCLE

The majestic Braviary can often be seen circling in Galar's skies. Write the even numbers from 12 to 28 in the circles so that the sum of the numbers in each straight line is the same. Two numbers have been completed for you.

FLIP OR FAIL!

Move the Poké Balls from the first pile to create the pile below.
Easy? You may only move THREE Poké Balls. Try sketching the
puzzle on a piece of paper.

FRIENDLY FACES

These friendly Pokémon are hanging out in the grid below. Find their names – they read forwards, backwards, up, down and diagonally.

B	U	C	F	Q	C	H	I	K	P
M	A	H	C	N	A	P	U	H	Y
U	R	A	K	I	T	L	O	J	X
N	W	R	X	O	E	U	B	I	R
C	Q	M	C	Y	S	H	Y	G	E
H	S	A	I	X	P	C	W	G	L
L	O	N	K	S	U	A	T	L	T
A	E	D	Z	F	R	K	O	Y	R
X	R	E	B	T	R	I	G	P	I
U	F	R	V	O	X	P	E	U	U
Y	L	P	Q	E	L	C	P	F	Q
J	P	F	I	W	E	M	I	F	S

CHARMANDER   JOLTIK   PANCHAM
EEVEE   MEW   PIKACHU
ESPURR   MUNCHLAX   SQUIRTLE
JIGGLYPUFF   TOGEPI

One little Pokémon is feeling shy! Rearrange the shaded letters to discover which critter it is.

— — — — — — —

START THE CLOCK!

Find a stopwatch or timer to record how long it takes you to solve the next teaser. Study the code on the Poké Ball carefully then fill in the missing letter. Think logically, Trainer, to avoid a headache like Psyduck!

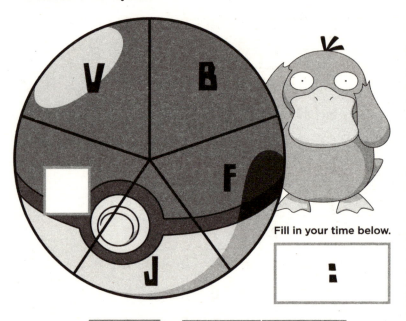

Fill in your time below.

:

QUICK QUIZ

1. Into which Pokémon does Psyduck evolve?

....

2. Tick the correct type for Psyduck.

3. Tick the two types Psyduck is weak against.

RIGHT RIOLU

This mini fighter is feeling muddled after a tough battle. Can you help revive it? Place the letters of its name – R, I, O, L and U – once each into every row and column of the puzzle. Identical letters must not touch, not even diagonally!

ON A ROLL

Help Ash solve this Poké Ball puzzle! If a Poké Ball contains a correct answer to one of the questions below, it will roll away. Do the maths to work out which Poké Ball is left at the end.

1. Poké Balls with a multiple of 4.
2. Poké Balls with a multiple of 5.
3. Poké Balls with a multiple of 9.

SHOCK TACTICS

Solve the riddle to meet a sparky creature that you should pat at your peril.

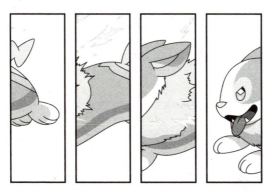

My first is in GROOKEY and also in PSYDUCK.

My second ends KIRLIA and GRENINJA too.

My third is in MEW and twice in MIMIKYU.

My fourth is in TOGEPI but never in TOGETIC.

My fifth is in BERRY but never in BURY.

My sixth is in FLARE but never in FLAME.

When you've solved the riddle, write out the name:

— — — — — —

MYSTERY MESSAGE

DIFFICULTY:

Team Rocket's tactics get sneakier and sneakier – now they are trying to hack Ash's computer! Scribble out the letter X every time it appears to decode the message.

XTXOXXDEXFEXAXTMXEXOXW
XTXHXXTXHXEXSXCXRXAXTX
CXHXCXXAXTXPXOXKXÉXMXO
XNXTXRXYXXUXSXINXGXAXFX
IXGXHXTXIXNXGX-XTXYXPEX.

Answer:

. . . .

. . . .

. . . .

. . . .

. . . .

CAUGHT IN THE MIDDLE

Attention, Trainers! Each four-letter word shown appears in the centre of a bigger word. Fill in the blank spaces to create the original word, revealing the name of a Pokémon, each time.

1. | | | P | O | R | E | | |

2. | W | O | O | L | | |

3. | | | | C | L | O | P | |

4. | | L | A | R | E | | |

5. | | R | O | O | K | | |

Look out for a Legendary answer this time!

6. | | M | A | Z | E | | | |

REAL DEAL

Hey Trainer, let's see whether you have the type advantage! Begin at the START, then follow a route to the FINISH, landing on only the true types. Avoid the fake ones or risk the wrath of a ravenous Munchlax!

START

STEEL	LIZARD	ELF	DOUGH
FAIRY	MOON	LEAN	GLITCH
POISON	SLUSH	WHEAT	DATA
PSYCHIC	NORMAL	IRON	BELL

FINISH

WEIGHING IN

What a buzz these Electric-type Pokémon are having! Study the
weight on each scale, then figure out how much Raichu, Jolteon
and Yamper each weigh by themselves.

54.5 kg

38.0 kg

43.5 kg

68.0 kg

Raichu weighs:	____ . ____ kg
Jolteon weighs:	____ . ____ kg
Yamper weighs:	____ . ____ kg

CRYSTAL CHALLENGE

DIFFICULTY:

Here's a problem that will chill you to the core – Team Rocket have been trying to clone Glaceon's ice crystals! Spot the true ice crystals that Glaceon has created – there's one unique crystal in each row to find.

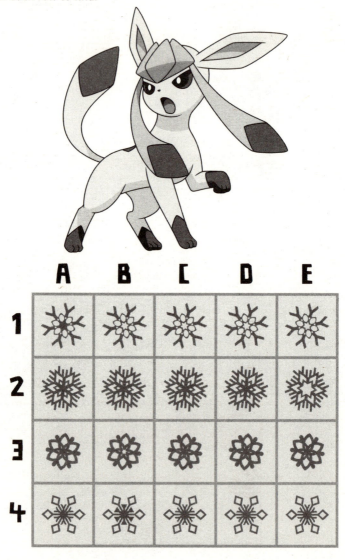

BUGGING OUT

DIFFICULTY:

Trace the paths to discover the name of a less-than-friendly
Bug-type Pokémon. Try to solve the anagram in your head
before tracing the paths.

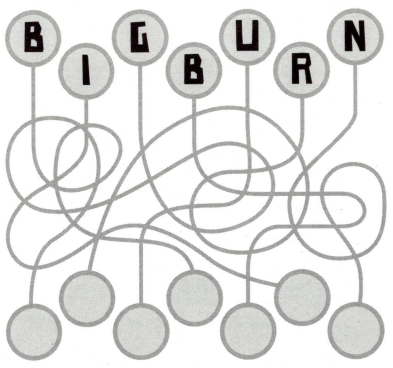

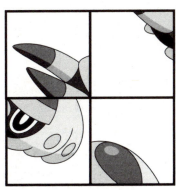

BINARY BIND

Ash is in a bind: he must re-programme his three computers using binary code. Help him fill in the blanks to get the computers working again.

RULES:

1. Each box should contain either a zero or a one.

2. More than two equal numbers immediately next to or below each are not allowed.

3. Each row and each column should contain an equal number of zeros and ones.

4. Each row is unique and each column is unique – any row cannot be exactly equal to another row, and any column cannot be exactly equal to another column.

COMPUTER 1

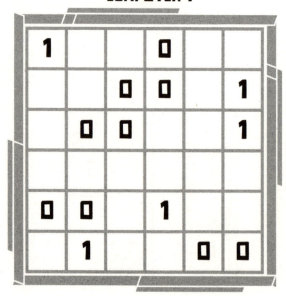

1			0		
		0	0		1
	0	0			1
0	0		1		
	1			0	0

COMPUTER 2

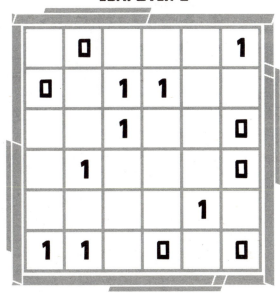

COMPUTER 3

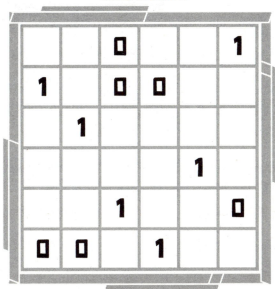

65

SOLUTIONS

FIRING UP

PAGE 6

The Pokémon's name is: CHARIZARD.

Some of the words that can be made include:
HAZARD, ACRID, CHARD, CHAIR, CAIRN, RADAR, CHIRR,
CHAD, HARD, HAIR, CHID, CARD, RICH, RAID, CZAR, ACID,
ARCH, ARID, CHAR, HAD, RID, RAH, HID, HIC, ARC, AIR,
AHA, CAR, CHI, AID.

THAT'S THE SPIRIT!

PAGE 7

1. C
2. A
3. C

The Pokémon evolve in this order:
1. Duskull
2. Dusclops
3. Dusknoir

PIKACHU'S PUZZLE

A	B	C	D	E	F	G	H	I	J	K	L	M
24	25	26	1	2	3	4	5	6	7	8	9	10

N	O	P	Q	R	S	T	U	V	W	X	Y	Z
11	12	13	14	15	16	17	18	19	20	21	22	23

The message reads:
Pikachu should use Quick Attack,
Iron Tail and Thunderbolt.

FEELING SQUARE

= 16

= 25

= 23

= 25   = 21   = 18

CRITTER COMBAT

PAGE 10

The word is: BATTLE.

GOLDEN SLUMBERS

PAGE 11

1. DEN, 2. CAVE, 3. TREE,
4. BURROW, 5. NEST.

Snorlax evolves
from Munchlax.

CRATES COUNT

PAGE 12

1. 9 crates. 2. 16 crates.

NINETALES' NUMBERS

PAGE 13

Puzzle 1:

3	8	4	6	1	5	7	2	9
9	7	5	2	8	4	3	1	6
2	6	1	9	3	7	8	4	5
1	5	6	7	2	3	9	8	4
8	9	2	4	6	1	5	3	7
7	4	3	8	5	9	2	6	1
5	1	8	3	9	6	4	7	2
6	3	7	5	4	2	1	9	8
4	2	9	1	7	8	6	5	3

Puzzle 2:

3	8	4	6	1	5	7	2	9
9	7	5	2	8	4	3	1	6
2	6	1	9	3	7	8	4	5
1	5	6	7	2	3	9	8	4
8	9	2	4	6	1	5	3	7
7	4	3	8	5	9	2	6	1
5	1	8	3	9	6	4	7	2
6	3	7	5	4	2	1	9	8
4	2	9	1	7	8	6	5	3

Tree 1: 50, +27, −4, ×3, ÷2, 18

Tree 2: 84, −4, ×8, ÷6, +16, 50

Tree 3: 363, +9, −46, ÷2, ×100, 8

WHO'S THAT POKÉMON?

Grookey.   C. Grass ✓

GROOKEY THE CHIMP POKÉMON IS CONFIRMED TO BE A GRASS-TYPE.

GROOKEY THE CHIMP POKÉMON IS CONFIRMED TO BE A GRASS-TYPE.

ON THE DOUBLE

PAGE 16

MEGA MORPH

PAGE 17

JOLT
MOLT
MOST
MIST
FIST
FAST

1. C. Charmander, A. Charmeleon, B. Charizard.
2. A. Sobble, C. Inteleon, B. Drizzile.
3. B. Bulbasaur, C. Ivysaur, A. Venusaur.
4. A. Machop, C. Machoke, B. Machamp.
5. C. Rhyhorn, B. Rhydon, A. Rhyperior.

PSYCHIC POWERS

PAGE 19

TASTY TREAT

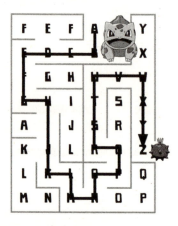

WHO'S THAT POKÉMON?

IVYSAUR

VENUSAUR

HIDING OUT

The coordinates are:

Woobat	B7
Larvitar	B3
Braviary	D6
Dusclops	G1
Mimikyu	E2
Onix	F5

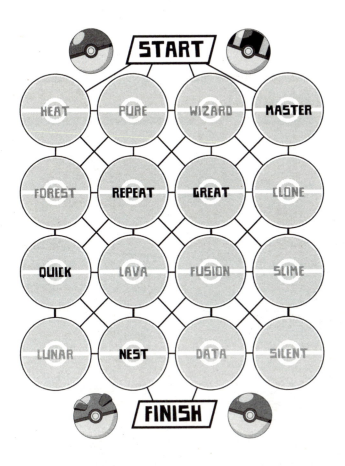

WEIGHT WORK OUT

PAGE 23

Pikachu weighs 6 kg, Munchlax weighs 105 kg
and Snorlax weighs 460 kg.

TALKING IN RIDDLES

PAGE 24

The word is:
MASTER.

GALAR GRID

PAGE 25

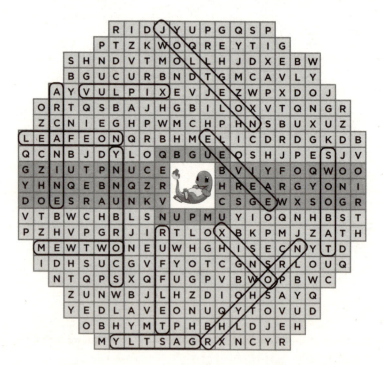

WHO'S THAT POKÉMON?

Charmander is hiding at the centre of the grid.

A. Fire

A FAIR FIGHT

PAGE 26

1. PANCHAM.
2. MACHOP.
3. GALLADE.
4. HAWLUCHA.

ON THE ATTACK

PAGE 27

Puzzle 1

N	X	I	O
I	O	X	N
X	N	O	I
O	I	N	X

Puzzle 2

I	O	N	X
X	N	I	O
N	X	O	I
O	I	X	N

A GASTLY PUZZLE

PAGE 28

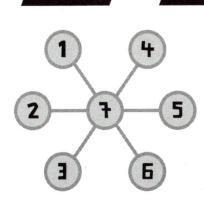

Total of each line = 14.

Other number combinations are correct – try 7, 4 or 1 in the centre.

B
L
A
S
T
O
I
S
E

V
L A P R A S
P
O
R M
F E E B A S
E G
O I
N K
A
D R E D N A W R   S O B B L E
P S Y D U C K   Q
W A R T O R T L E
I
T
L
E

A	B	C	D	E	F	G	H	I	J	K	L	M
Z	Y	X	W	V	U	T	S	R	Q	P	O	N

N	O	P	Q	R	S	T	U	V	W	X	Y	Z
M	L	K	J	I	H	G	F	E	D	C	B	A

The message reads:
MEOWTH CAN BE
DEFEATED BY CHOOSING A
FIGHTING-TYPE POKÉMON.

TRIPLE TEST

PUZZLE 1

PUZZLE 3

PUZZLE 2

(T) (U) (R) (F) (E) (L) (F)

(R) (U) (F) (F) (L) (E) (T)

CREATURE COPY

The Pokémon's
name is:
BUTTERFREE.

Bug- and Flying-type

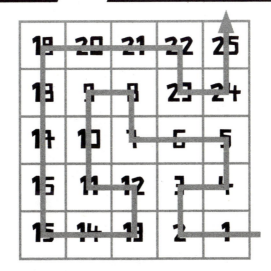

IN THE DARK
PAGE 36

Shadow E was cast by the
Pokémon, which is DEINO.

WHO'S WHO?
PAGE 37

1 D
2 E
3 B
4 C
5 F
6 A

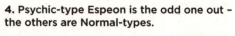

ODD TYPE OUT
PAGE 38

1. Ghost-type Dusknoir is the odd one out –
the others are Fire-types.

2. Fairy-type Alcremie is the odd one out –
the others are Fighting-types.

3. Grass-type Grookey is the odd one out –
the others are Water-types.

4. Psychic-type Espeon is the odd one out –
the others are Normal-types.

5. Normal- and Fairy-type Jigglypuff is the
odd one out – the others are Electric-types.

PUZZLE 1 = 27 triangles.

PUZZLE 2 = 35 triangles.

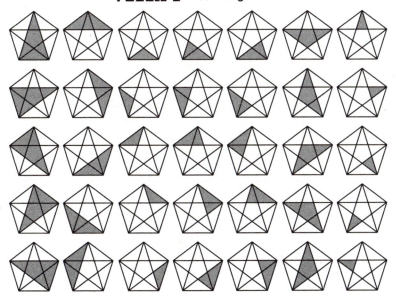

CHAIN REACTION

PAGE 40

1. A. Squirtle, C. Wartortle, B. Blastoise.
2. C. Caterpie, B. Metapod, A. Butterfree.
3. B. Pichu, A. Pikachu, C. Riachu.
4. C. Gastly, A. Haunter, B. Gengar.
5. B. Deino, C. Zweilous, A. Hydreigon.

WINGED WONDER

PAGE 41

The word is: DRAGON.

LEGEND HAS IT

PAGE 42

The Legendary Pokémon is: ZAMAZENTA.

Some of the words that can be made include:
MEANT, AMAZE, MEAN, ZETA, NAME, MANE, MEAT, META, MATE, MAZE, NEAT, TEAM, AMEN, ANTE, TAME, NET, TEA, MET, TAN, TEN, MEN, ATE, ANT, EAT, ETA, MAN, MAT.

IN A TANGLE

PAGE 43

C O N G E A L

G L A C E O N

FIRST CATCH

PAGE 44

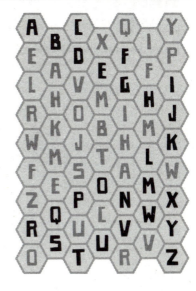

The Pokémon is: MACHOP.

FIRST CATCH

PAGE 45

The Pokémon is: MACHAMP.

RACE DAY

PAGE 46

Since Lapras beats Magikarp, Squirtle beats Lapras and
Psyduck beats Squirtle, Psyduck is the winner of the race.

LEAFEON'S TEST

RAVEN RIDE

PAGE 48

The Pokémon is:
CORVIKNIGHT.

The word that
isn't real is:
UNKNIGHTED.

ASH'S QUEST

HERO
HERD
HEAD
HEAR
FEAR
FEAT

CRITTER CHALLENGE

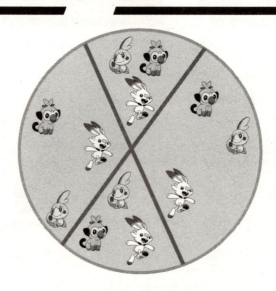

PAGE 51

FULL CIRCLE

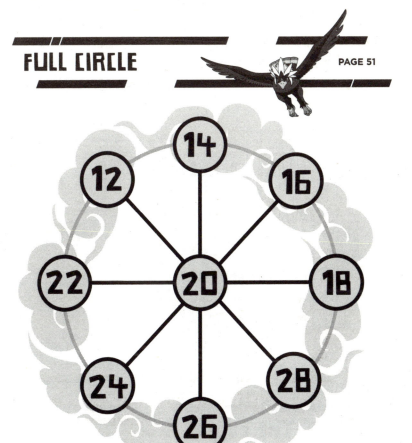

PAGE 52

FLIP OR FAIL!

FRIENDLY FACES

B	U	C	F	Q	C	H	I	K	P
M	A	H	C	N	A	P	U	H	Y
U	R	A	K	I	T	L	O	J	X
N	W	R	X	O	E	U	B	I	R
C	Q	M	C	Y	S	H	Y	G	E
H	S	A	I	X	P	C	W	G	L
L	O	N	K	S	U	A	T	L	T
A	E	D	Z	F	R	K	O	Y	R
X	R	E	B	T	R	I	G	P	I
U	F	R	V	O	X	P	E	U	U
Y	L	P	Q	E	L	C	P	F	Q
J	P	F	I	W	E	M	I	F	S

The shy
Pokémon is:
PICHU.

START THE CLOCK!

Each letter follows a vowel in the alphabet.

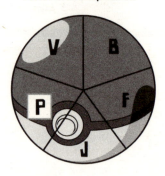

QUICK QUIZ

1. Psyduck evolves into GOLDUCK.

2. Psyduck is a WATER-TYPE Pokémon.

3. Psyduck is weak against GRASS and ELECTRIC-TYPE Pokémon.

RIGHT RIOLU

PAGE 55

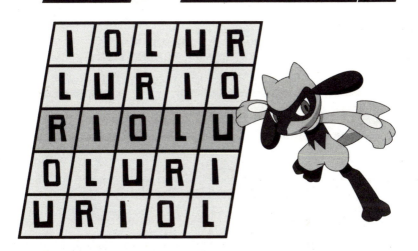

ON A ROLL

PAGE 56

Multiples of 4 = 4, 8, 12, 28
Multiples of 5 = 25, 45, 50
Multiples of 9 = 9, 18, 27, 45, 54, 63, 99

The Poké Ball that is left is:

SHOCK TACTICS

PAGE 57

The Pokémon is:
YAMPER.

The message reads:
TO DEFEAT MEOWTH THE SCRATCH CAT
POKÉMON TRY USING A FIGHTING-TYPE.

CAUGHT IN THE MIDDLE

PAGE 59

1 V A P O R E O N

2 W O O L O O

3 D U S C L O P S

4 F L A R E O N

5 G R O O K E Y

6 Z A M A Z E N T A

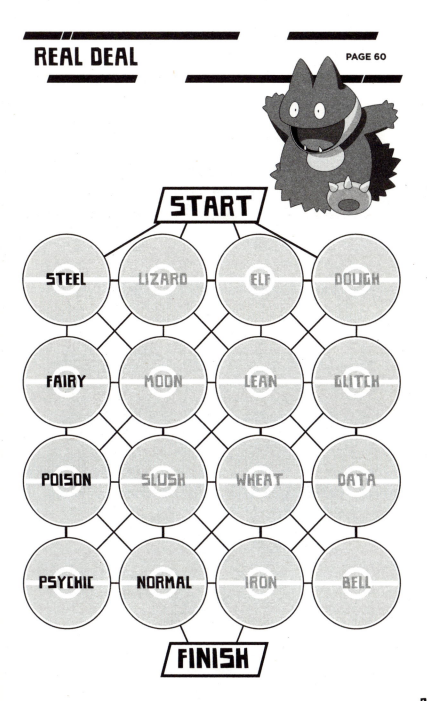

START

STEEL — LIZARD — ELF — DOUGH

FAIRY — MOON — LEAN — GLITCH

POISON — SLUSH — WHEAT — DATA

PSYCHIC — NORMAL — IRON — BELL

FINISH

WEIGHING IN

Raichu weighs 30.0 kg, Jolteon weighs 24.5 kg
and Yamper weighs 13.5 kg.

CRYSTAL CHALLENGE

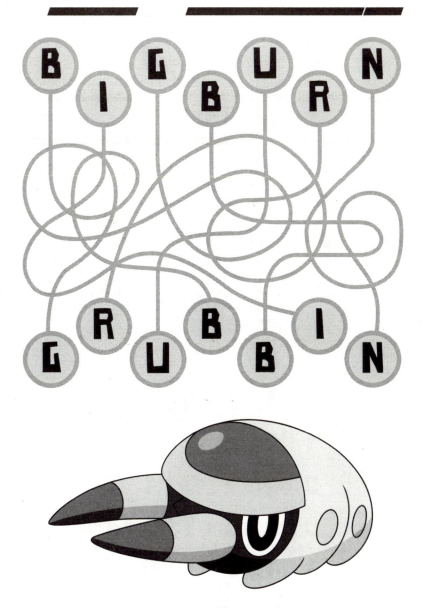

COMPUTER 1

1	0	1	0	1	0
0	1	0	0	1	1
1	0	0	1	0	1
0	1	1	0	1	0
0	0	1	1	0	1
1	1	0	1	0	0

COMPUTER 2

1	0	0	1	0	1
0	0	1	1	0	1
0	1	1	0	1	0
1	1	0	1	0	0
0	0	1	0	1	1
1	1	0	0	1	0

COMPUTER 3

1	0	0	1	0	1
1	1	0	0	1	0
0	1	1	0	0	1
1	0	0	1	1	0
0	1	1	0	1	0
0	0	1	1	0	1